Lake Michigan

Great Lakes of North America

Harry Beckett

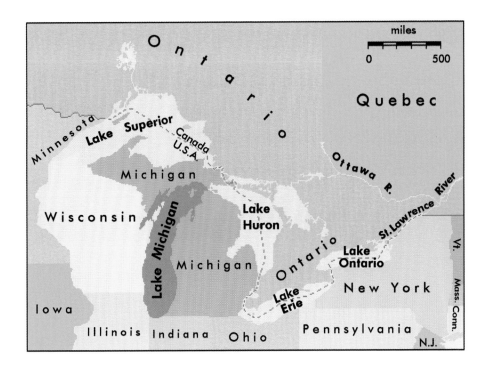

The Rourke Corporation, Inc.
Vero Beach, Florida 32964

PHOTO CREDITS:
Photographs by kind permission of: Wasaga Beach Provincial Park;
National Archives of Canada; Wisconsin Division of Tourism
Geovisuals, Waterloo, Ontario; Wisconsin Maritime Museum; Chicago
Convention and Visitors bureau; Michigan Sea Grant; Fort Mackinac State
Historic Park; Collingwood Museum, Collingwood, Ontario; Maps by David
J. Knox

CREATIVE SERVICES:
East Coast Studios, Merritt Island, Florida

EDITORIAL SERVICES:
Susan Albury

Library of Congress Cataloging-in-Publication Data

Beckett, Harry, 1936-
  Lake Michigan / by Harry Beckett.
    p. cm. — (Great Lakes of North America)
  Includes bibliographical references and index.
  Summary: Discusses Lake Michigan's geography, history, early
inhabitants, important events, economy, and more.
    ISBN 0-86593-524-6
  1. Michigan, Lake Juvenile literature. [1. Michigan, Lake.] I. Title. II.
Series: Beckett, Harry, 1936- Great Lakes of North America.
F553.B43 1999
977.4—dc21
                                                    99-13023
                                                    CIP

Printed in the USA

TABLE OF CONTENTS

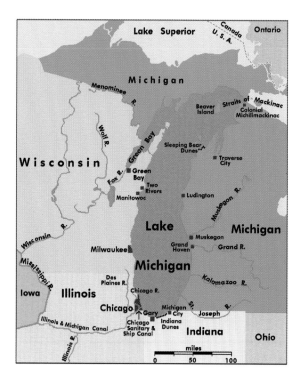

FACTS AND FIGURES FOR LAKE MICHIGAN

Length	307 miles	494 kilometers
Width	118 miles	190 kilometers
Average depth	279 feet	85 meters
Maximum depth	925 feet	282 meters
Volume	1,180 cubic miles	4,920 cubic kilometers
Water surface area	22,300 sq. miles	57,800 sq. kilometers
Shoreline (inc. islands)	1,638 miles	2,633 kilometers
Area of basin	45,600 sq. miles	118,000 sq. kilometers
Height above sea level	577 feet	176 meters
Retention time*	99 years	

* The average time that it takes for a molecule of water to enter and leave the lake.

ABOUT LAKE MICHIGAN

Lake Michigan has the third largest surface area of the five Great Lakes and is the only one that lies entirely within the United States. It is bordered by Michigan (east and north), Wisconsin (west), Illinois (southwest), and Indiana (southeast). The lake is regular in shape, except where Green Bay cuts into Wisconsin in the northwest. A hundred or more rivers and streams feed the lake.

Among the most important rivers are the Muskegon, Grand, Kalamazoo, and Saint Joseph, which flow in from the east, and the Fox-Wolf and the Menonimee which empty into Green Bay. The Chicago River used to flow into the lake at the southern end, but engineers reversed its direction in 1900. It now flows out of the lake through the Chicago Sanitary and Ship Canal into the Des Plaines River, and through the Illinois and Michigan Canal into the Illinois River, all part of the Mississippi River system. The waters of Lake Michigan circulate slowly in a counterclockwise direction and flow out at the northern end into Lake Huron through the Straits of **Mackinac** (MACK in aw).

The land around the lake is low and rolling, with wide beaches and rocky cliffs jutting into the lake. Wind and water action have piled up huge sand dunes at spots along the western Sunrise Shore, which is otherwise quite rugged.

A Michigan Historic Site

LAKE MICHIGAN

This lake, the sixth largest in the world, was discovered in 1634 by Jean Nicolet, who explored this north shore to Green Bay but found no Orientals as the French in Quebec had hoped he would. The general size and outline of the lake was established in the 1670's by Marquette and Jolliet. They named it Lake Michigan. Its elongated shape was an obstacle to transcontinental expansion, but its waters soon proved a real boon to commerce.

MICHIGAN HISTORICAL COMMISSION REGISTERED SITE NO. 120

The dunes in Sleeping Bear National Park, near Traverse City, and in the Indiana Dunes National Lakeshore and State Park on the southeastern shore, the highest dunes in the world, are an important tourist attraction. The north shore is heavily forested and sparsely populated, and has most of the lake's islands, including the largest, Beaver Island. The southern shore has rich farming areas, large settlements, and busy industrial developments.

Sand dunes at Sleeping Bear National Park (Michigan).

NATIVE PEOPLES AND EARLY EXPLORERS

Nomadic (no MAD ik) peoples that we call
Paleo-Indians were already hunting caribou, musk ox
and woolly mammoths in the Lake Michigan area as the
last ice age retreated. At the first European contact, the
Menominee lived a **sedentary** (SED un tair ee) life,
chiefly by gathering wild rice, on the present Michigan-
Wisconsin border. The Winnebago and the Fox lived in
eastern Wisconsin, though many Fox were killed and the
rest driven out when the Ojibwa obtained firearms in
about 1690. The Potawatami lived east and west of the
lower lake, and the Illinois, Kickapoo, and Miami lived at
its southern end. Ottawas from the Michilimackinac area
acted as traders between the nations.

Jean Nicolet was looking for a land route to the Pacific when he landed near Green Bay in 1634. He thought that he was in the Orient and amazed the Winnebago welcoming party by stepping ashore wearing magnificent Chinese robes. Other explorers soon followed—Louis Jolliet and Père Marquette, who mapped Michigan's western shore, René-Robert Cavelier de LaSalle, and Pierre Esprit Radisson and Medard Chouart des Groseilliers. By 1710, fur traders were moving into the rivers and forests of the western shore. Their arrival attracted Ojibwa, Ottawa, Huron, and others who drove out older inhabitants—the Winnebago, Kickapoo and Fox.

In 1667, Nicolas Perrot established a fur-trading post at Green Bay and claimed the area for France. It passed into British control after the French and Indian Wars (1754-1763), and then became U.S territory after the War of 1812. Better travel routes attracted waves of settlers who came into conflict with Native peoples. This led to the Black Hawk War (1813), and the **suppression** (suh PREH shun) of the indigenous peoples. To the south, the conflict ended in the defeat of the Native Americans at the Battle of Tippecanoe (1811).

The Native Americans of Wisconsin are proud of their traditions.

Jean Baptist Point Sable, a French-Haitian, was the first settler in the Chicago area, around 1779. European settlers came later to the eastern shore. Protestant missionaries arrived in the Traverse City area in 1838. Although the land belonged to the Native peoples, a law was passed in 1845, forcing them to give it up if white settlers demanded it.

After leaving Green Bay, La Salle went on to explore the Mississippi River all the way to the Gulf of Mexico. (From a 1904 calendar)

Towns and Cities

Chicago, the United States' third largest city, stretches 29 miles (46 kilometers) along the lakeshore and its **metropolitan** (meh truh PAH luh tun) area (population 7,687,191) reaches from the Wisconsin border into Indiana. The site was important long before it was settled. A short **portage** (por TAHZ) from the Chicago River opened up a route to the south.

Chicago's lakefront, with its parks and beaches, is designed for recreation. Science, art, and history museums, buildings by leading architects, a world-famous symphony orchestra, and winning sports teams prove the city's motto, "I will."

Three of the world's ten tallest buildings are in Chicago, and the world's first skyscraper was built there fourteen years after the Great Chicago Fire of 1871. Chicago is nicknamed the "windy city" because the shape of the lake acts like a funnel, channeling winds southward.

Milwaukee (population 628,088) began as a Native American gathering and trading center and became a North West Company fur-trading post. It grew rapidly with the arrival of many German refugees after 1848. Marquette University, named for the explorer who visited the area in 1673, and the Wisconsin Conservatory of Music are among its many fine colleges and educational institutions. Milwaukee has major league basketball and baseball teams.

Green Bay is the oldest permanent settlement in Wisconsin and the gateway to the Midwest through the Fox and Wisconsin Rivers. The Green Bay Packers, one of America's major football teams, took its name from the city's meatpacking industry.

The U.S. Steel Company built Gary, Indiana (population 116,646), on land west of the Indiana dunes that it had bought for the iron ore and coal beds which lay under it.

Lake Michigan is a part of the city of Chicago.

Other places include Muskegon, Grand Haven, Traverse City, and Michigan City. A car ferry service between Ludington and Manitowoc saves many hours of driving around the lake. The ice-cream sundae was invented in Two Rivers, near Manitowoc, in 1881.

The lakefront in Milwaukee, Wisconsin's largest city

WORKING AROUND THE LAKE

Lake Michigan's economy is based on manufacturing and **service industries** (SUR vuhs IN duhs treez) and on the **processing** (PRAH ses ing) of raw materials. A wide network of railroads, highways, waterways, airlines, and gas and oil pipelines connects at the south end of the lake. Ships and barges from the Saint Lawrence Waterway or from the Mississippi River arrive with bulk cargoes such as coal, oil, grain, and iron ore. Industry turns this material into steel, machinery, engines, automobiles, and other manufactured products, or processes it into pharmaceuticals and petrochemicals that are shipped out to the lake ports and beyond.

Grain from the Midwest also passes through Milwaukee, famous for its beer. The Lake Michigan basin area produces a third of the United States' steel (until recently, Gary was the nation's leading steel producer), much of it for the automobile industry. Many large companies and financial institutions have head offices in Chicago.

The Lake Michigan states have strong agricultural economies. They are producers of fruit and vegetables, as well as large numbers of cattle. Wisconsin is known as America's dairyland and is a major producer of hogs and eggs. Meatpacking and food processing are important industries. The warming influence of the lake allows apples and cherries to be grown as far north as Traverse City.

After the fur trade, settlers turned to the forests for timber to build towns and ships. In the late 1800s, Muskegon, "the city that built Chicago and a hundred other prairie towns," had 47 sawmills. Not many years later, the timber was running out due to poor forestry management but the lumber, pulp, and paper industries have remained important in cities such as Green Bay, thanks to better forestry management and reforestation.

The beauty of the shoreline brings tourists to Lake Michigan.

Tourism, based on the beautiful beaches, heritage buildings, and traditional crafts, is a major industry. Commercial and recreational fishing, once major activities on the lake, were almost wiped out by lamprey eels. The restocking of the lake trout population and the introduction of coho salmon is reviving the industry.

Fruit orchards are a common sight around Lake Michigan.

DISASTERS AND MYSTERIES

On October 15, 1880, a side-wheeler called the *Alpena* was sailing in beautiful weather for Chicago when, in one hour, the temperature fell 33° F (18° C). Winds of 70 miles per hour (112 kilometers per hour) drove heavy snow squalls across the lake and whipped up huge waves. No one knows what happened to the *Alpena* and the seventy to eighty people on board. Only a few pieces of wreckage were ever found.

The *Alpena* was not the only vessel lost on the lake in the three days of what is now known as the Alpena Storm. Ninety-four vessels were damaged or wrecked, and one hundred and eighteen people lost their lives. Twenty vessels were wrecked within 50 miles (80 kilometers) of each other.

The greatest disaster on Lake Michigan was not caused by a storm but by human error and bad luck. The excursion steamer *Eastland* was popular for its lake cruises. Early in the morning of July 24, 1915, two thousand five hundred people were crowded aboard. Most of them were on the upper decks and on one side of the ship, watching the activities on the dock. A lack of communication between the captain and the crew caused the ship to roll onto its side, trapping passengers below the waterline and killing eight hundred and thirty five.

The tug Favorite *alongside the* Eastland.

The 217-foot (66-meter) steamship *Chicora* left Milwaukee at 5 AM on an unusually fine January 21, 1895. If it had sailed ten minutes later, it would have received word that the barometer was falling fast. The *Chicora* was about halfway across the lake when a fierce winter storm roared in. The vessel was never seen again. Two bottles were found months later with messages from the desperate crew but underwater searches have failed to find the wreck or the crew.

The Chicora

INTERESTING PLACES

Twenty-eight submarines and over a hundred other vessels—minesweepers, landing craft, and submarine chasers—were built in Manitowoc during World War II. Local leaders and former submariners wanted to recognize the town's part in the war effort, so they founded the Manitowoc Maritime Museum. The U.S. Navy donated the U.S.S. *Cobia*, a submarine of the type built in the town. Later the museum was expanded to cover the maritime history of all the Great Lakes and to commemorate the town's shipbuilding history that began almost a century before.

The first wooden ship was launched in Manitowoc in 1847. By 1900, more than two hundred vessels had been built at as many as ten shipyards.

At the museum, now called the Wisconsin Maritime Museum, visitors can walk the streets of a historic Great Lakes port, see a reproduction of a section of an 1854 clipper ship, view a collection of detailed model ships, and, if they are lucky, spend the night aboard the *Cobia*.

The Straits of Mackinac (MACK-in-aw) was a traditional gathering place for Native people long before the first Europeans entered the area. Today, costumed **interpreters** (in TUR pruh turz) relive 1770s life at Colonial Michilimackinac, a restoration of the old colonial crossroads. Michilimackinac is the native name for *turtle*, which has been shortened to *Mackinac*. Cannon drills and black-powder musket firings boom and crack around the reconstructed fort.

The U.S.S. Cobia

Outside the walls, local Native people show how a Native-American village of that time worked, and there is even an eighteenth-century wedding. In a unique underground "Treasures from the Sand" exhibit, archaeological **artifacts** (AHR teh fakts) from over 275 years of settlement are on display.

Close by are Mackinac Island with its famous fort and historic Mill Creek, one of the Great Lakes' first industrial sites, where **sawyers** (SAH yurz) give demonstrations of pit-sawing and a water-powered sawmill in operation.

A diving suit on exhibition at the Wisconsin Maritime Museum

GLOSSARY

artifact (AHR teh fakt) — something made by human work or art

interpreter (in TUR pruh tur) — a person who acts a role to show how life was

metropolitan (meh truh PAH luh tun) — with all the suburbs and small towns that surround a chief city

nomadic (no MAD ik) — moving from place to place, looking for food, etc.

portage (por TAHZ) — a route between waterways where the canoe must be carried

process (PRAH ses) — to prepare or treat

sawyer (SAH yur) — a person who works in a sawmill

sedentary (SED un tair ee) — settled in one place

service industry (SUR vuhs IN duhs tree) — work that supports the public or other industries (e.g. transport)

suppression (suh PREH shun) — crushing, putting down

Soldiers load their muskets with black powder and shoot.

INDEX

FURTHER READING

You can find out more about the Great Lakes with these helpful books and web sites:

- James P. Barry. *Wrecks and Rescues of the Great Lakes,* Howell-North
- *The Great Lakes, an Environmental Atlas and Resource Book*
  Got. Of Canada and USEPA
- J. Morley and D. Antram. *Exploring North America,* Peter Bedrick Books
- Gilbert Legay. *Atlas of Indians of North America,* Barron's
- Pierre Berton. *The Great Lakes,* Stoddart
- Chicago Office of Tourism ci.chi.il.us/Tourism
- Great Lakes MARITIME Museums, Societies and Resource Centers, Box 7365,
  Bowling Green, OH 43402
- Chambers of Commerce of Traverse City, Muskegon, Milwaukee, Manitowoc
- Wisconsin MaritimeMuseum

- www.d.umn.edu/seagr
- www.great-lakes.net
- Quizzes about the Great Lakes: www.hcbe.edu.on.ca/coll/lakes.htm